Stop the Propaganda Machine from Controlling How You Think and Vote

A Blueprint for Detecting Deception

Dr. Mel Whitehurst

"What good fortune for those in power
that people do not think."
Adolf Hitler

CONTENTS

1
WHAT DO YOU BELIEVE?

"We are in the greatest crisis in the history of our country."

"The American people need hope."

"Our government is a disaster."

"I will restore the American dream."

"Terrorists are the real threat to our country."

"We need to return to conservative government."

"We cannot keep overspending and creating budget deficits. We have to govern responsibly."

"I will support universal healthcare."

"My goal as a congressman the next four years is to destroy the president."

"If elected, I will go after Wall Street and break up the big banks."

"I'll shut down the government if necessary because it is the will of the American people."

"We need to send our military into the Middle East and wipe out the terrorists."

"The President is in a secret conspiracy with antigun groups to take our guns away."

"Social Security and Medicare will be bankrupt in ten years if we don't act now."

"On the first day of my presidency I will eliminate Obamacare."

"We should carpet bomb the terrorists into oblivion."

"We have to build a border wall or our country or be overrun with criminals and rapists."

"Liberals are taking away our liberty."

"We need a president that leads, not one that is out of touch with the American people."

Have you heard any of these statements by political leaders before? Which statements do you agree with? How does each statement make you <u>feel</u>? With which statements do you most agree and with which do you most disagree? Do you believe political leaders really believe the statements they are making or are they just "hyping" us to get our vote? How do we know the real political issues? Are some simply manufactured problems to control us to think and vote a certain way?

It is difficult and complex to ever really know if political leaders are telling the truth. In this book, I present several deception-detecting strategies that can be utilized to sort out statements for truth. Current political issues are identified and explained to demonstrate the role they play in deception. I show numerous persuasion tactics political leaders use to convince us to think and vote the way they want us to think and vote and describe how <u>not</u> to get caught up or, more concisely, controlled, by the drama of political leaders' communications to persuade us to vote for them without at least making a smart effort to understand the real messages. Along with truthful communications often come lying, spin, hype, hate-speech and fear-mongering. However, the truth really matters. We have the responsibility as voters to do what we can to learn the truth. Deciding what is truthful and what is deceptive takes considerable effort.

I trust that most political leaders (including political candidates) start out with honest and straightforward political agendas they think represent the views of voters. As these views are challenged by others, a typical reaction is to dig in, become defensive and instigate strong persuasive tactics to gain and maintain support. Hence, the ensuing attempts at controlling our thinking and voting.

Most of the information in this book comes from my work experience as a psychologist for more than forty years, 27 of them in private practice. I also acquired information by carrying out several mini social psychology research projects as you will see when you read the book. Of course, I conducted extensive examination of psychological research journals. And, recently I've been talking to my family dog, Rocky Bob. He's a good listener and it's surprising what one can learn from a good listener when writing a book.

Looking at the Problem

Political leaders and the mass media collaborate in a business relationship to build a giant **Propaganda Machine** which collectively consists of newspapers, internet, radio, and television. Political leaders who seriously want our vote use the **Propaganda Machine** in attempts to tell us how to think and vote by delivering enormous amounts of influence messages to us at an unrelenting pace. The lightning fast speed of sending these messages makes it possible to keep us in information overload and causes us to have only enough time to briefly consider the extensive volume of information. To simplify the array of information coming to us, I focus on what I consider to be the more influential elements of the **Propaganda Machine**: selected internet online news websites, front pages of selected newspapers and fact-check websites.

Political leaders' willingness to invest immense amounts of money in using the news media for delivery of messages demonstrates that we are being successfully controlled to think and vote the way political leaders say we should think and vote. Otherwise, they would not be expending these vast financial resources.

Consensus opinion regarding our American democracy declares that our government is under the control of the people who vote. Political leaders diligently identify voters' wants and needs by getting input from them, and then strive to represent these wants and needs after they are elected to political offices. Voters' issues therefore shape leaders' actions. That is the way our democracy is supposed to work. With development of the **Propaganda Machine** the role has been reversed. Political leaders regrettably have moved toward autocratically selecting political issues and in collaboration with the news media, campaign to convince us to think and vote the way they decide we should think and vote.

Frustration with political deception displayed through the **Propaganda Machine** has led to a substantial escalation of distrust among voters. Voters have become angry and skeptical resulting in the dramatic rise of cynicism and doubt toward our government.

Voters should be shaping political leaders instead of political leaders shaping voters. But, this requires an informed activist voter. We need to sort through the **Propaganda Machine's** communications to distinguish fact from fiction, to vote actual concerns instead of manipulated opinions, and to select political leaders who are effective in creating a collaborative and cooperative voter-led government. When we vote for political candidates who support our actual issues, not issues programmed into us, we help create a collective decision for selection of the political candidate who fully represents the issues of the greatest number of people. (3, 4, 16, 17)

Warning

An enormous amount of money is spent researching how to influence and persuade us. Those running for political office seek supporters and promotion money, employ experts in campaign and influence management, and organize and carry out strategies to get us to think and vote the preferred way of the political leaders. Regrettably, political leaders readily use untruths if they believe it will influence us, and mostly adhere to the maxim that "the end justifies the means" when campaigning for office.

Political leaders are primarily motivated to get elected. The news media is motivated to send messages through the **Propaganda Machine** that attracts customers and the subsequent advertisers, which, in turn, provides them with more profits. There is nothing inherently wrong with these motives. I simply wanted to point out that we should be aware that political leaders and the **Propaganda Machine** can have underlying and differing motives to influence us to think and vote other than what we may expect.

2

THE STATE OF OUR CURRENT DEMOCRACY

Democracy is the best form of government ever created. Informed democratic voting is far superior to any other form of government. American democracy, because of its immense success, has lead the way for other democracies to be established throughout our planet. However, with the phenomenal rise of the **Propaganda Machine** in America, voters daily receive distorted and biased messages, which leads them to make misinformed choices that subsequently place political leaders in office who do not adequately represent the actual voter issues, therefore leading toward a less efficient government and the ongoing and rising discontent among our general population. Finding the truth before voting will lead to more effective democratic decision making.

The Free Press

The free press plays a crucial role in maintaining an open and free democratic society, and cannot be compromised without severe loss of our freedoms. My observation is that the free press, in its competitive quest for news and with the proliferation of innovative news collecting and reporting technologies, has been gradually compromised over the past fifty years. There is less and less objective and balanced reporting. Furthermore, the free press is being manipulated by political leaders to focus on influencing voters' thinking and voting behavior rather than reporting in an objective and balanced manner.

This has to change! Members of the free press have to stand up and report the news uncompromisingly so that voters can comprehend the motivations and will of our political leaders. Political leaders need to report to the voters. We need to know who is funding them and to whom they are actually reporting or we run the ominous risk of allowing a few heavily capitalized lobbying groups or individuals to dictate the political agendas.

Why We Vote

We are inclined to vote for candidates who support our values. Consequently, for our vote to count, we have to be able to vote for those who will support our genuine values.

Voter values are generally known by those seeking political office. For example, it is known that voters on the right tend to value safety, harmony and stability of individuals in society, respect tradition, commitment, and acceptance of ideas that culture or religion provides, dislike actions that harm others, and control over people. (28) Voters on the left value universalism and identity with the entire population of the planet rather than with an individual country. Understanding, tolerance and protection of the welfare of all people were more important than to those on the right. (12, 20, 23, 33, 34) If there is a significant difference between our values and political leaders' agenda, political leaders agendas' will override voters' values.

Political leaders know from behavioral research that we will be motivated to vote our emotions, that is, we are more than likely to vote based on how we feel about an issue instead of what we think about an issue. (6) Consequently, focus will be on eliciting positive and negative emotions such as anger, fear, enthusiasm, and pride as a way to control our thinking and voting. (16, 27) Further, political leaders know that if anxiety can be evoked within us, we will pay more attention to political races and will vote in higher numbers. (7) Hence, generating anxiety among voters is a vote getter.

Interestingly, candidates running behind in political races usually try to provoke the negative emotions of fear and anger while candidates running ahead will aim at the positive emotions of enthusiasm and pride. (24, 27) These strategies by candidates seem to be successful. (27)

Of course, there are other reasons we vote. We are apt to vote when we feel a threat exists and a political settlement is the way to eliminate the threat. Threat produces a greater voter turnout. If we are unhappy because we think an injustice has occurred, we will almost certainly vote for candidates that appear to extract the most revenge. (Behavioral research reveals that given the opportunity, most of us are generally more than happy to seek revenge.) (5) Warlike candidates are attractive to voters who think injustices have occurred.

Is It Really Necessary for Most People to Vote?

If we choose to live in our democratic society, it is our personal responsibility to vote. We have an obligation to contribute. Democracies decline and society-wide problems increase when people become indifferent to selecting their political leaders. Lack of participation opens societies to more authoritarian and dictatorial leaders who can ultimately take away many of our freedoms. Declining to vote because we suppose our vote does not count is a specious justification for indolence and negligence. Voting takes effort and every vote counts.

3
EMERGENCE OF THE GIANT
PROPANDA MACHINE

*Let me recap my previous contentions. A giant **Propaganda Machine** exists. Political leaders collaborate with the mass media to create the machine. Both the political leaders and mass media receive reciprocal benefits from their business relationship, which may or may not benefit the voter.*

The **Propaganda Machine**, which represents and reports for political leaders, includes a variety of information technologies. I chose only to examine communications as reported in four selected internet news websites, the front pages of four newspapers and four fact-check websites. News websites and newspapers' front pages were divided in half, two with a conservative slant and two with a liberal slant.

I set out first to identify themes from the most frequently reported news articles in internet news websites and front pages of newspapers by examining 750 news articles over a three-week period. (See Table 1 for entire list of themes.) The five most reported themes were politics, crime, terrorism, economy, and violence. It is noteworthy that when combined, crime, violence, and terrorism accounted for over 34% of all the reported news themes; themes which represent destructive behaviors toward other humans. There should be no doubt as to why we spend billions of dollars each year on the military, police protection and personal home security systems to protect ourselves with crime, violence and terrorism taking center stage.

Next, I reviewed 67 news articles that focused directly on themes expressed most often by political leaders. The economy, terrorism, gun control, and morality/religion were the most reported themes of political leaders, which I might note was relatively dissimilar to the priority themes reported in 750 news articles reviewed. (See Table 2 for complete list.)

Is it possible that political leaders are misaligned and out of touch with the actual issues? Comparison of differences between reported themes in news websites and newspapers with the themes of political leaders gives me some indications of disagreement between reported political themes and the themes reported by political leaders. A future study might provide some interesting information on how well political leaders are "tuned in" to voters. But, from a cursory examination, my review of news article themes shows a problem-disconnect between voters and political leaders!

Additionally, I studied 78 news articles that were fact-checked by four fact-check websites to determine which political issues politicians were most truthful and most untruthful. (See Table 3) Political leaders tended to lie more about healthcare, the economy, crime, and international relations and to tell the truth more often about gun control and immigration. I am not sure what this means, but I have a subtle feeling that telling untruths indicates lie-tellers either have no solutions to the issues or they fear loss of voter approval. Again, it would be interesting to know why leaders are truthful and untruthful on important voter issues.

Last, and perhaps most important, I identified the persuasion tactics political leaders used to influence us to think and vote by reviewing 80 news articles. Fifteen persuasion tactics were identified. They are listed in rank order in Table 4. Fear-appeals, accusations and attacks, calls to action and declarations of winning are the most commonly used tactics. My general sense is that political leaders with more extreme political ideologies, right or left, used fear-appeals, character assassinations and spin and hype more often.

Persuasive Tactics of Political Leaders

Below I describe fifteen persuasion tactics that I detected my media study. I list them in rank order based on frequency of use, beginning with the most frequent, fear-appeals. (See Table 4 for rank order)

Fear-Appeals

Fear-appeals are statements that things are "really bad" or "getting worse." Declarations designed to instigate gloomy feelings that something bad is happening or about to happen are the cornerstones of fear-appeals.

I know from my previous research that fear is being programmed into our minds at an alarming rate. Last year I conducted an eight-week semi-scientific fear study. I reviewed 424 randomly selected news articles from three national news networks, three cable news networks, two internet news websites, the front page of a newspaper, editorials and letters to the editors. I classified the negative news articles as fear-based and found that 78.30% of all the stories reviewed were fear based.

Fear-appeals from the **Propaganda Machine** are tremendously effective in convincing voters to vote a certain way. Political leaders frequently use fear-appeals to raise our personal threat level so they can energize us to take action directed by the political leader. Once we become fearful, our attitude, intentions, and behaviors are easy to manipulate. Fearfulness will stop us from being open-minded and will frequently cause panic, self-protectiveness, and distrust. (30)

Political leaders who portray themselves as the leaders who have solutions to our fears will likely get our vote because the solutions are going to reduce our fears. I've seen considerable amounts of behavioral research showing that fear inducement coupled with a solution to the fear is a very efficient vote getter. (18, 32)

Accusations and Attacks

Accusing and attacking another person or group as doing something clandestine or committing an action that is considered wrong was used at a high frequency. Finger pointing attacks place the problem onto something or someone else and provide us with someone or some issue to vote against.

We are Losing

Competing and winning is a highly esteemed value in our American culture. The majority of people do not like to be thought of as losers. Statements that we are failing or being defeated by the opposition will motivate us to vote for the candidates who convince us they will compete and win.

Call to Action

A statement calling for action to be taken will provide us with a sense of empowerment. We will always feel stronger when we take action. Taking action, even a failed action, is superior to doing nothing and feeling vulnerable. Voting thus becomes an empowering act because it helps us believe we are doing something to resolve a problem rather than sitting around and feeling helpless.

Logical/Factual Appeals

Using logic or facts to support political issues appeals to our reasoning. Appealing to our reasoning with logic and facts can induce us to make a "reasoned" step to vote for a political candidate. The difficulty is knowing when logic or facts are sound, whether it is our logic or their logic.

Discrediting

Discrediting statements indicate that another person is personally inept or uninformed in some way. Doubts of competence are stated. Voters, in general, have a strong tendency to believe discrediting statements even when they have no substance. Discrediting will motivate us to get rid of the demeaned person and vote for someone else.

We are Winning

A statement that says we are succeeding or thrashing the opposition, and the person making the statement is the prime instigator of winning, can cause us to vote for them because we all want to get on the bandwagon of success.

Spin and Hype

Hype is exaggerating a truth to magnify the importance of the truth. Spin is revising interpretation of events to make them more positive. Consider the following spin example:

> A Russian newspaper reported that the Russians and Americans were in an international car race. The Russian car finished second and the American car finished next to last. (The spin: There were only two cars in the race.)

Political leaders commonly employ public relations firms specializing in spin and hype to gain voting support. Public relations organizations are highly skilled in putting a spin or hype on just about any political issue.

Voters oddly love spin and hype. It has drama. It's exhilarating. Voters get "cranked up" when politicians add this kind of pizazz to their speeches. Paradoxically, voters will readily open themselves to manipulation by spin and hype.

Reinterpreting Past Actions

Reinterpreting past actions to support present views is a

way to get our vote. The past is unalterable, but political leaders can change their interpretation of what happened. Deftly reinterpreting history to aggrandize a political leader's agenda is commonplace. Watch out for reinterpretations because it may be hard to know about a political leader's real past actions.

Morality Claims

We will vote for a worthy moral cause over nearly anything else. Examples are: individual liberty, respect for authority, individual responsibility, altruism, caring for others, and other factors that define good and bad. Morality issues generally appeal to our moral goodness with words such as patriots, "real" Americans, flag waving, loyal Americans, good ole American values, liberty, peace, truth, freedom, peace, hope, happiness, security, caring for others, etc.

Religion is a common morality issue. (30) Although religions in America differ in the values they emphasize, there is a central agreement that being religious will make a better life for the individual and a better society. Words such as religious values, God fearing Christians, loyal Christian Americans, God's will, etc. are used. (31, 38) A political leader who professes to be religious gets more votes.

Lying

Lying is so commonplace that it is accepted as a natural part our culture. We all tell lies when the lies serve us and when the probability of getting caught is low. (1) We may not be consciously aware that we are telling lies much of the time, especially the small "inconsequential" lies such as "Good morning, how are you?" "I'm fine, thank you". How many times have you told someone you were fine when you were not? Political leaders can get caught up in telling people what they want to hear without being aware that they are telling a "small" lie. These lies are the most stealthy and problematic to recognize.

Because of this prevalent human behavior, we have to be astute in ferreting out lying by political leaders as they try to influence our thinking and voting. If we do not want to be manipulated, it is our responsibility to decide which issues portrayed by candidates are counterfeit and which are truthful.

Political leaders know that if they tell a lie repeatedly, we will eventually believe it no matter how preposterous it is. If political leaders want voters to believe a lie, they simply tell it over and over. Moreover, voters are gullible to the "big" lie, so a big lie is the best lie! (1, 10, 25, 26)

The extent to which political leaders keep their campaign promises is another area where lying flourishes. Voters rarely pay close attention to whether political leaders fulfill their commitments. One study found that members of congress voted their campaign promises only 73% of the time. (22) Repetitively making the same promise is usually enough to convince us to vote for them. Political figures know that we seldom hold them accountable for their promises.

Political leaders occasionally employ what I refer to as the first lie maneuver, where they deliberately provide misinformation, information that is not completely true, and then follow up at a later date with an apology and correction of the communications knowing that voters tend to remember only the initial false information rather than the correction. They can lie and correct the lie as a mistake later and get away with it. Don't be the victim of believing the first lie maneuver! (25)

We are more than likely to accept lies from political leaders we like, even when we know the truth is not being presented. Regrettably, voters habitually support and stand up for politicians that are lying because they like them! (10)

Good-hearted and conscientious people are more gullible and tend to readily believe others with less discernment. Moreover, they have more difficulty in detecting lies. (9) I cited this to show that regardless of our insightfulness and astuteness, we are all vulnerable to other people telling lies. We have to be attentive to detect lying among political leaders and through the **Propaganda Machine.**

I decided to review some behavioral research to find out how the best lie tellers in our society tell lies, and discovered some interesting information from lie-telling criminals. Criminals know that human deception detection ability is generally ineffective and that people can easily be manipulated with lies. The ensuing information describes some of the lie-telling strategies used by criminals. (28)

Stay close to the truth in telling a lie. Truths are easier to remember.

Keep the lie simple. A short and simple lie has less details and is therefore easier to remember.

Include descriptive details. Details give a lie plausibility.

Keep eye contact. Tell the lie looking directly at the camera.

Appear direct and forthright.

Keep calm and relaxed. People who look and act anxious are always suspicioned.

Act as if you believe the lie.

Tell lies and truths in the same manner. Be consistent.

Evading an issue or question is a common lie tactic of political leaders. Hedging may seem innocuous: "More research is needed..." "A fact-finding committee is working on the issue..." "I am calling for an investigation on this failure," etc. Passing the issue to another authority allows political leaders to lie by omission.

Does the truth really matter? As shown by a behavioral researcher, people will stand up more forcefully for political beliefs that cannot be proven factually than for beliefs that can be demonstrated precisely by facts. (11) Does this mean that our most valued political beliefs are emotionally-based and irrational? Could it be that political leaders who stay with the factual truth will have a greater chance of failing? Could it be that the political conflicts and dysfunctions are intensified and worsened by leaders who stay with non-factual unproven political beliefs?

I believe the truth matters. It is our responsibility as voters to do what we can to not be manipulated or deceived by deception and lying.

Character Assassination

Attacking an opponent's character rather than the issue is away to plant doubt in voters' minds. Name calling such as "liberals", "hippies", "progressives", "radicals", "extreme right-winger or extreme left-winger", "Nazi", "Special interest group", "tree hugger", "radical", "racist", etc. can brand an opponent without facts to back up the accusation.

If political leaders can create an enemy with clever character assassinations, then they can save us from the enemy with campaign assurances.

I/We Will Destroy You

Statements that the political leader will destroy an

opponent can lead voters to feel more secure. Voters love leaders who take <u>power-oriented</u> stances.

Standing Tall Aggressively

People admire political leaders that appear to stand up to some "evil doer". Most voters appreciate political leaders who aggressively stand up for an issue or value. Of course, aggression does not always lead to the solving of problems, but we voters love people who "stand up" to someone or something.

Everybody is Doing It

People are motivated to follow other people's behavior. We have a tendency to determine what is or is not effective by observing and comparing ourselves with others. Once we see others taking actions we have an inclination to believe they are correct.

People tend to follow the most popular course of action even when it may be more harmful than helpful. (6, 8, 9) Get on the bandwagon statements, "This is the will of the people", "Speaking for the American people", etc. are persuasive. Testimonials from respected or famous people are commonly used by political leaders. A majority of people, even when confronted with an erroneous majority opinion, will ignore the contradictory evidence of their own and agree with the majority. Statements that indicate the majority wants a course of action or that a majority is already pursuing a course of action are powerful vote getters.

4

STRATEGIES FOR DETECTING DECEPTION

<u>American voters vote the way they are told!</u> Sounds like I am declaring that we are mindless sheep being led by shepherding political leaders. Actually, I am implying this somewhat, but not absolutely.

There are more attempts at influencing us than at any other time in history. We receive multiple messages every day from political leaders via the news media telling us how to think and vote. It is so routine that we probably do not notice the impact it is having on our thinking and voting. We are highly likely to be unintentionally thinking and voting the <u>exact</u> way political leaders are telling us to think and to vote. Unless we prefer to remain submissive followers we will have to devote more energy to deciding for ourselves how we will think and vote.

As previously emphasized, the intent of this book is to provide ways to stop becoming a voter victim of distorted political persuasion tactics and subsequently to cast a well-informed vote, a vote that actually means something. Below, I will describe strategies to detect the truth or falsity of written information being relayed to us by the **Propaganda Machine** from political leaders who want to control our thinking and voting.

Detect and diminish deception with two-sided reasoning.

Every politically-oriented written article has two points of view. The vast majority of voters quickly make up their minds about which side of the political issue they want to be on and generally do not take the time to thoroughly look at the other side. If we can comprehend both sides of a political issue, we have a better opportunity to discern truthfulness. After understanding both sides, we will have an improved view on how to vote for the political leader who will best represent us.

Understanding both sides of a political issue requires deliberate employment of <u>empathy</u>, the ability to adopt another person's point of view and to think and feel like the other person while, at the same time, staying separate. Empathy is one of the most important of all human skills.

We may disagree on a political issue, but through empathy should be able to see and perhaps comprehend a different point of view. Empathy is not agreeing with the other point of view, however. We are only dropping one point of view briefly and attempting to grasp the opposite point of view.

Empathy is learned by practice. Consistently practice empathizing with others—seeing their point of view. Observe what happens when we attempt to see another person's point of view nonjudgmentally while carefully refraining from agreeing with it. Becoming skilled enough to routinely see two sides of an issue will lead us to make more competent voting decisions.

Another way to learn empathy is to deliberately identify the two sides of an issue in a written article. (There is always two sides.) Read the article and identify each side of the issue. Experience one side of the article as if total agreement. Then reverse the process by agreeing with the other side. When we complete this task we should be able to see more clearly the two-sided point of view. Last, pick the side of the issue that <u>feels</u> most agreeable and go with it as the preferred side.

This is a very simple and brief process, but I know that when anyone can see both sides of any issue, their decision making ability is greatly enhanced.

(Note) There are literally hundreds of experimentally designed studies which demonstrate that highly empathic people have greater interpersonal and decision making skills, are less prone to depression and anxiety, not easily manipulated and swayed, and more successful in their careers. (Among psychologists, empathy is considered the skill most essential to becoming a therapist.)

Establish a progressive skepticism mindset.

Progressive skeptics are scattered throughout all American political parties, democrats, republicans, and independents. Progressive skeptics are probably in the majority, although we frequently fail to get our way in politics because progression is change and change is not always easy to implement. Nevertheless, I firmly believe that progressive skeptics in all political parties are the citizens who have advanced our American way of life in the past and will continue to do so in the future.

Progressive skeptics possess a mindset that questions most of the things they read and hear. They view political leaders and news media communications with skepticism and curiosity.

Fundamentally, progressive skeptics believe that political issues are never static. Issues are always changing and evolving and are either getting better or getting worse. Hence, they take the stance that anything can be improved or made better and that we are better served when we concentrate on evolving positive-oriented solutions and stay away from rigid negative-oriented solutions. For example, downsizing government, cutting taxes, or reducing the federal budget are not areas progressive skeptics will primarily concentrate on because these political issues are negative-based.

Progressive skeptics believe that by focusing on positive solutions to improve our government they will be able to resolve problems and, in the process of doing so, will diminish the difficulties of high taxes, overstaffed government bureaucracies, and budget deficits.

Upholding a progressive skeptic mindset will help us identify the political leaders who will solve problems instead of only complaining about them. Use the following questions to compare and contrast the mindset of progressive skepticism with non-progressive skepticism.

Progressive Mindset

Does the political leader propose understandable positive solutions?

Does the political leader support his/her views with evidence and facts?

Does the political leader "feel" believable?

Non-Progressive Mindset

Does the political leader propose or emphasize eliminating or reducing a problem, without suggesting a solution?

Does the political leader attack or accuse someone or a group of wrong doing, without suggesting a plausible solution?

Does the political leader emphasize that things are bad and getting worse without suggesting a solution?

Does the political leader take a moral stance which implies others do not uphold morality in some way?

Does the political leader give the aura of negativity?

I believe the progressive skeptic mindset is a way of thinking which leads to better deception-detection as well as effective voter decision making.

Look for the political leader who leads us to feel more optimistic and hopeful and less cynical and pessimistic.

Favor the political leader who instills a sense of hope within us. Try this. Form the habit of visualizing political leaders in your mind and then observe how you feel about them. If it is a good feeling, you should probably vote for the political leader. If it is a bad or cluttered feeling, you will need more information to decide on the candidate to make an effective vote.

We are more vulnerable to voting for a political leader espousing a cause when the cause is one of our causes.

People will work harder for a cause than for money. It is easy to overlook political leaders' incompetence when they support our personal causes. Political leaders are aware of the role of causes and frequently espouse causes for which they do not actually believe, but know that holding on to the cause will get votes. Be attentive to this.

Stay especially cautious in voting for political leaders who define their political platforms as potential loss.

More problems get solved when defined as a potential gain. When a situation is described in terms of a potential gain, we are more likely to take action than when the problem is described in terms of what we stand to lose. For example, if a political leader shows how his/her economic plan will ultimately benefit the most Americans this is defined as a potential gain. On the other hand, if his/her economic plan is described in terms of what Americans will lose if the plan is not implemented this is defined as a potential loss. (6)

The use of anger.

Political leaders who use anger and urge voters to get angry about a political issue will eventually raise the overall level of anger among the voters they are trying to influence, possibly to a point where the anger, not the issue, dominates. <u>Expressing or venting anger will not reduce anger</u>. Research clearly shows that expressing anger actually raises the level of anger and that few problems are solved in an anger-state. Once again, I emphasize, remain aware of the political leader who uses anger and encourages voters to get angry about something. Persistent anger eventually stops all progress or causes disintegration of efforts. Observe the anger-blocking behavior of our congressional representatives for the past several years!

Political leaders who encourage us to take specific actions to solve political problems will be the most effective leaders.

Vague and general solutions are a smokescreen for inaction by political leaders. Democracy gets stronger when more and more people take action. The very act of doing something changes things.

More often than most of us believe, we will obey authority.

We rarely challenge political leaders. Complain about them maybe, but challenge them, no. Although we may well give a substantial amount of attention to those who "challenge" the status quo or challenge authority, unfortunately, we will probably end up obeying an authoritarian leader. Stop mindlessly accepting authority until their authoritarian declarations and behaviors have been rationally challenged. We need democratic leaders who can accept and respond to challenges, not autocrats who resist or avoid challenges. (2, 6, 20, 21,)

Become an evolving voter instead of an entrenched voter.

Keep an open mind to altering belief(s) after logically examining them. Most people, when directly confronted with proof that their beliefs are wrong, do not generally change their beliefs or course of action or even examine them, but justify their beliefs even more tenaciously. Keep an open mind. (6)

Look for trends in political communications.

Some political leaders may trend negative, using fear and negativity as ways to motivate you to vote for them. Others trend positive to secure your votes. Some political leaders are balanced. Negative trends usually trigger fight or flight behaviors. The political leaders are either encouraging you to stand up and fight or to withdraw from an issue. Positive trends are associated with political leaders urging you to make a situation better. While negative and positive trending may have its advantages, I believe political leaders with a balanced approach are the best leaders. Take some time to assess the trending patterns of political leaders. (14)

Be cautious of opinion polls.

Opinion polls have been growing in numbers the past few years and there is evidence from research that these polls influence our vote. (22) Voters dislike being associated with losing, so they have a propensity to jump on the "bandwagon" of whoever is leading in the polls. The research indicates that a substantial number of voters tend to support candidates leading in the polls when they might have supported another candidate if the poll data were different. The power of polls, especially if they are not scientifically validated, could lead us to selecting the most ineffective political leaders. Make a concerted effort to focus on the candidate while at the same time challenging the result of polls to formulate our own validity. (22, 13) Don't let the "bandwagon effect" decide for you.

Be cautious of a political leader who takes an extreme left or extreme right position.

Political leaders with extreme positions may be correct in their approach and may have justifiable reasons for taking these extreme positions, but history shows that significant deviations from an accepted practice requires a greater amount of strategy development, support, and implementation efforts to achieve the change, and rarely do political leaders completely succeed with extreme approaches. Radical change will be more disruptive and voters often resist change even if it helps them! Those with extreme positions seldom accomplish their goals unless it is done incrementally. Look to see what extreme position holders have for an incremental plan to achieve their goals. Do not completely dismiss extreme change, however. The change plan or strategy to accomplish the change is critical. Observe carefully how the change agent political leader plans to accomplish the change, a key component to extreme change. (37)

Use intuitive thinking.

Using intuitive thinking to find the truth or deception in information produced by the **Propaganda Machine** is one of the best ways to determine if a political leader is "real" or just manipulative. Employing intuitive thinking is actually learning to trust our instincts. Here is how we can go about doing this.

Thinking can be divided into two categories: conscious and unconscious. Conscious thinking operates knowingly in our awareness while unconscious thinking operates without conscious control and cannot be brought easily to our awareness. We can deliberately control the sequence and direction of the conscious thinking through logical thinking, but not the unconscious thinking.

Our unconscious thinking is referred to as intuitive thinking. Intuitive thinking is constantly processing and categorizing information at an unconscious level, and then for some unknown reason making part or all of it available to consciousness.

Intuitive thinking is correct most of the time if you take the time to understand it. Problems with intuition arise when we misinterpret the information. The objective is to recognize intuitive information when it comes to our conscious awareness and then to correctly interpret it.

When we read a newspaper article, our conscious awareness is logically analyzing the article while at the same time the unconscious is conducting an analysis below our level of awareness and may be sending signals to our conscious awareness as to the result of this unconscious analysis.

Unconscious messages usually appear in our conscious awareness in one of the following ways:

- Hunches, gut feelings, and impressions. The feeling that something is wrong or something is lacking in a situation---things just do not feel right. Or, an instant good feeling that something is right.

- A sudden solution appears at an unexpected moment and everything seems to fit together.

A primary way to connect with our intuitive messages is to deliberately pay attention to how we **feel** when reading news media communications concerning political leaders or political issues. For instance, if when reading an article about terrorism, a sudden negative feeling comes to our awareness, but we are not sure why, we should stop and focus on the feeling. Instead of suppressing the feeling or just automatically reacting, fully experience the feeling, then step back and logically analyze the feeling. Logically explore the feeling, speculating as to what it means. If we take this approach in responding to intuitive feelings, we will gradually become more skilled at recognizing, validating, and responding to these formidable unconscious messages.

Fully experience both positive and negative feelings when they come to conscious awareness. While I believe a negative feeling will provide us with valuable information, a positive feeling can also provide meaningful information.

Our unconscious can also provide us with a sudden solution or answer to a political issue. Psychologists call this the "click phenomenon", when instantly all the elements of an answer to a political issue come together in a solution and arrive in the conscious mind from the unconscious mind. I dare say that we've all had experiences where we have a sudden solution to a problem that feels like the right answer but are not certain as to why. If an unexpected immediate insight arrives from our unconscious containing a solution to a problem, we can apply logical thinking to evaluate the solution.

In summary, logical thinking is the process of reasoning to reach a conclusion. If a sudden feeling comes to our consciousness, decide what the feeling is telling us. Speculate and generate ideas, then make a decision as to what it is really telling us to do or not to do. If a rapid solution comes from the unconscious, speculate on the impact and consequences of the solution. If the impact is negative, drop the solution and if it is positive, pursue the solution.

To refine intuitive skills consider practicing the following for several days. Each day make a conscious effort to pay attention to your feelings or any slight doubt that unexpectedly comes into your awareness. Also, be alert to any sudden insights into solutions to problems or in seeing the whole picture for the first time. If you are uncertain as to what these feelings or insights mean, apply your logic to speculate as to what their significance may be. You may be right or wrong on your speculation, but if you consistently do this you should gain increased insight into what your intuitions mean and how to efficiently use them. Deliberately being more aware is a simple and easy process that enhances your ability to find truth in political media.

Watch the motivations of political leaders closely before voting.

If we want to make an accurately informed vote, we should develop some reasoned thoughts as to the primary motivations of the political leaders. It is relatively easy to identify motivations observing a few key surface behaviors of political leaders.

I place motivation into three categories: Power Motivation, Achievement Motivation and Affiliative Motivation. (19) Each of these three motivations can be positive forces for political candidates. Below is a criteria to assess the three motivations.

Power Motivation

Power motivation is the desire to control other people for one's own goals or to achieve goals for the greater good of the whole. Some examples of power motivated political leaders...

They are more focused on what "I" will do than what "We" will do.

They remain autocratic in solving problems instead negotiating solutions.

They make power-oriented statements and talk "tough": Example: "We will smash our enemy," or "We will stand up to them."

They frequently use accusations, attacks, character assassinations and discrediting as influence tactics.

They consistently advocate determined and forceful actions.

Achievement Motivation

Achievement motivation is the desire to excel and to achieve goals. Some examples of achievement motivated political leaders...

They frequently talk about goals.

They use "We" statements more often than "I" statements.

They provide details of future and actions.

Affiliative Motivation

Affiliative motivation seeks to have harmonious relationships with other people. Some examples of affiliative motivated political leaders...

They will tend to conform and shy away from standing out.

They will seek approval rather than recognition.

They emphasize working together with all factions.

They talk about getting approval from voters frequently.

They prefer statements with the words, "The American Public believes..."

<u>Behavioral research suggests that presidents with a high power motivation make the best presidents initially</u>! Presidents first have to secure power before achievement because government is about "shared" power. Once a president has secured enough power he/she will shift toward achievement. Have you noticed how presidents take strong actions the last year or so before exiting? They've accumulated more power to act by their last days in office.

Unless political leaders can get their share of power, they will not be able to make meaningful accomplishments while in office. (29, 35, 36) Observe how political leaders are attempting to gain power and decide for yourself if they are succeeding. I know that most of us think of attaining power as always bad, but most of the time, political leaders who gain power use it for the good. Powerlessness is more dangerous in political leaders. In every strata of our society, it is the powerless that are most destructive to themselves and others, and the same holds true for powerless political leaders.

Write a letter.

An excellent way to find out how a political leader will respond to voters is to write a letter to the political leader requesting more clarification on a particular political issue that is important to you. You will likely get a written response perhaps from the political leader's assistant or even a standardized response letter. Even when the leader does not personally write the letter, the leader is still responsible for overseeing communications. Analyze closely the reply. How did the reply make you feel? The written reply will tell you a lot about a political leader and whether the leader is willing to <u>engage</u> in two-way communications with a voter. If an election campaign is under way, write a letter to all candidates and see what happens.

A few years ago, I wrote a letter to my state senator about an issue important to me. I had been a supporter of this political leader in the past. The return letter I received was basically insulting, even though I had merely asked a question for clarification of an issue. The political leader must have assumed I was opposing something. As you can guess,

I never again voted for this political leader nor did I provide any future campaign support. In fact, I conducted my own small retaliation campaign by telling this story to at least twenty of my friends and attempting to discourage them from voting for the candidate in the future. I'm glad I wrote the letter because I found out about how the political leader responded to a "lowly" voter.

Write letters and engage political leaders in a dialogue. Stand up to them and ask questions. Don't back down. Your one votes counts equally and just as much as the CEO of the largest corporation in America.

5

THOUGHTS ABOUT MY THOUGHTS

I often have thoughts about my thoughts. Some call this meta-thinking. My friend, Elrod, calls it second guessing. Anyhow, looking back over this book, I have some "second" thoughts to express.

I'm gullible every now and then. I tend to believe the political leader who is enthusiastic, smiles a lot and communicates in lucid sound bites. It's hard for me to challenge a cheery communicator. To complicate this, I really want to believe that people will always tell the truth. Combining my naïve trust of happy politicians and desire to believe complicates finding out who to believe.

I often feel pushed to get in line with the "program" after reading a compelling political message. I pay special attention to the push from "outraged" political leaders. No matter what their political persuasion, when they get angry, I return the anger by getting angry at them for being angry. Anger for me is a very intimidating emotion. I have friends who simply do not pay attention to any political message. To them, all political messages are meaningless. It's not worth their time. I think they are dangerously wrong.

No doubt, unquestionably, absolutely, I believe the <u>wealthy</u> run our country. <u>And, the rest of us go along with them.</u> After all the wealthy are smarter and know more than us mere underlings. They must be smarter to be able to get all that money (my rationalization). At least that is my humble view. I sometimes fight them back in my <u>mind</u>. I love the underdog who rises up to fight for her/his cause. I am annoyingly attentive at how the wealthy-elite also rise up and smash these little fighters who are standing up for their cause. On rare occasions the underdog wins!

Truth in politics is whatever you want it to be. It is situational. It changes by the minute. If I published the three previous statements on the front page of the newspaper, I would probably be confronted by groups of people who believe there are absolute unchanging truths in the world and that I am misguided by some sinister being. They could be right. There may be some unchanging truths in the world....but not in politics.

I admire consumer advocates and political writers who "challenge" others. They are few in number and are always skating on a tenuous platform. Nevertheless, they make a powerful difference. I recently attended a presentation by a consumer advocate. I made the decision after seeing the presentation to become my own personal advocate. Hope I don't get sued.

I've always prided myself in being a logical and rational person, but when it comes to making voting decisions my feelings decide for me. I'm not certain of the role logicalness and rationality anymore. Perhaps it comes first before the feelings. All the same, I still think being logical and rational is the best way to go in voter decision making.

I dislike authoritarian political leaders. In fact, I fear them. I still don't know how to effectively challenge authoritarian political leaders even though I think they need to be challenged. I've always been the person who holds the coat while someone else jumps into the authoritarian's arena and scraps with them. I've got to change this. I will do it after we get through the next election. Meanwhile, I'll hold your coat.

Part of the requirements of becoming a counseling psychologist back in graduate school (a long time ago) was to participate in a sensitivity training group, a form of group therapy designed to make doctoral students more aware of themselves and others. It was an "all out, no holds barred" encounter group. Absolute honesty was required and demanded. It was both the most disconcerting experience of my life and the best experience of my life to that point. It taught me to think for myself, to look inside myself and rely on what I felt and thought. I've not been successful in doing this 100% of the time over the years but I have been successful most of the time. I find that when I do practice self-honesty as I learned in the group, I'm better at detecting lies and deception. And, I also sleep better at nights.

During my 40 plus years in counseling, I have witnessed almost every dark behavior human beings can exhibit, and I have spent countless hours talking with clients to help eradicate these detrimental behaviors. I have been face-to-face with the most destructive people among us and have seen firsthand horrifying evil being played out. Yet, at nearly the end of my long career, I see people overall as more positive than when I started. <u>It is wise never to underestimate political leaders' capacity for good.</u>

6
CONCLUSION

A dynamic political world in our American democracy is out there seeking to control how we think and vote. Democratic leaders want our vote and support. That is a legitimate pursuit. Their campaign to obtain votes is an integral part of our governing in a free and open society, and will continue to function to keep us strong as a nation.

Information communicated by our political leaders through the free press is absolutely essential if we are to remain a formidable democracy. The problem arises because not all information is accurate or truthful. We have to be individual thinkers and voters who think and vote our own views rather than manipulated views. I hope the information I provided in this book will help you toward becoming a more independent thinking and voting citizen and a better deception-detector.

APPENDIX A
INFORMATION SOURCES

Primary Sources
Dallas Morning News
Fox News-Latest News
Hot Air
Huffington Post
MSNBC
New York Times
Wall Street Journal
Washington Post
snopes.com
politifact.com
fact checker-Washington Post.com
factcheck.org

Secondary Sources
USA Today
Google

TABLE 1
RANKED SUMMARY OF HEADLINE TOPICS

Politics	154
Crime	107
Terrorism	97
Economy	80
Violence	55
International Relations	50
Climate	43
Healthcare	39
Morality/Religion	29
Technology	17
Court	13
Education	12
Human Interests	10
Race Relations	7
Gun Control	7
Energy	4
Military	4
Climate	3
Security	2

Number of Headlines Reviewed = 750

TABLE 2
RANKED PREDOMINANT POLITICAL
ISSUES OF LEADERS

Terrorism	20
Gun Control	18
Morality/Religion	15
Economy	4
Healthcare	2
Violence	2
Immigration	2
Crime	2
International Relations	2
Race Relations	0
Drugs	0
Social Security	0
Human Interests	0
Climate	0
Court	0
Education	0
Energy	0
Climate	0
Technology	0
Military	0
Security	0

TABLE 3
TRUTHFUL-UNTRUTHFUL HEADLINE CLASSIFICATIONS

	Truthful	Untruthful
Healthcare-Health Related	5	7
Terrorism	1	3
Immigration	3	2
Crime	1	8
Economy-Economic	8	14
Gun Control	1	1
Morality/Religion	0	2
International Relations	6	14
Court	0	1
Education	0	1
	N=25	N=53

Reviewed 78 Fact Checks   32.05% Truthful   67.95% Untruthful

TABLE 4
RANKED SUMMARY OF PERSUASION TOPICS

Fear-Appeals	20
Accusations and Attacks	17
We are Losing	13
Call to Action	11
Logical/Factual Appeal	8
Discrediting	8
We are Winning	7
Spin and Hype	5
Reinterpreting Past Actions	5
Morality Claims	4
Lying	3
Character Assassination	2
I/We Will Destroy You	3
Standing Tall Aggressively	3
Everybody is Doing It	2

Number of Identified Tactics = 111

Number of Reviewed Articles = 80

SOURCES

1. Arielly, Dan, **The (Honest) Truth About Dishonesty: How We Lie to Everyone—Especially Ourselves**, Harper Collins Publisher, New York, New York, 2012.

2. Bond, Robert, Fariss, Christopher, Jones, Jason, Kramer, Adam, Marlow, Cameron, Settle, Jaime & Fowler,James, **A 61-Million-Person Experiment in Social Influence and Political Mobilization**, Nature, 2012, Vol. 489, 295-298.

3. Capara, Gian Vittorio and Zombardo, Philip, **Personalizing Politics: A Congruency Model of Political Preference**, American Psychologist, 2004, Vol. 59, No. 7, 581-594.

4. Caprara, Gian Vittorio, Vecchione, Michele, and Schwartz, Shalom, **Why People Do Not Vote**, European Psychologist, 2012, Vol. 17(4), 266-278.

5. Carlsmith, Kevin, Wilson, Timothy, & Gilbert, Daniel, **The Paradoxical Consequence of Revenge**, Journal of Personality and Social Psychology, 2008, Vol. 95, No. 6, 1316-1324.

6. Cialdini, Robert, **Influence**, Fifth Edition, Pearson Education, New York, New York, 2009.

7. Civettini, Andrew & Redlawsk, David, **Voters, Emotions, and Memory**, Political Psychology, Vol. 30(1), 2009, 125.

8. Cohen, Geoffrey, **Party Over Policy: The Dominating Impact of Group Influence on Political Beliefs**, Journal of Personality and Social Psychology, 2003, Vol. 85(5), 808-822.

9. Elaad, Eitan & Reizer, Abira, **Personality Correlates of the Self-Assessed Abilities to Tell and Detect Lies, Tell Truths and Believe Others**, Journal of Individual Differences, 2015, Vol. 36(3), 163-169.

10. Fazio, Lisa, Brashier, Nadia, Payne, Keigh & Marsh, Elizabeth, **Knowledge Does not Protect Against Illusory Truth**, Journal of Experimental Psychology: General, 2015, Vol. 144(5), 993-1002.

11. Friesen, Justin, Campbell, Troy, & Kay, Aaron, **The Psychological Advantage of Unfalsifiability: The Appeal of Untestable Religious Political Ideologies**, Journal of Personality and Social Psychology, 2015, Vol. 108, No. 3, pp 515-529.

12. Frimer, Jeremy, Biesanz, Jeremy, Walker, Lawrence & MacKinlay, Callan), **Liberals and Conservatives Rely on Common Moral Foundations When Making Moral Judgments About Influential People**, Journal of Personality and Social Psychology, 2013, Vol. 104(6), 1040-1059.

13. Gilovich, T. and V. Medvec, V.H. "**The Experience of Regret: What, When, and Why,**" Psychological Review, 1995, 102, 379-395.

14. Gonzalez, Kirsten, Riggle, Ellen & Rostosky, Sharon, **Cultivating Positive Feelings and Attitudes: A Path to Prediction and Ally Behavior, Translational Issues in Psychological Science**, American Psychological Association, 2015, No. 4, 372-381.

15. Graham, Jesse, Haidt, Jonathan & Nosek, Brian, **Liberals and Conservatives Rely on Different Sets of Moral Foundations Journal of Personality and Social Psychology**, 2009, Vol. 96,(5), 1029-1046.

16. Harder, Joshua & Kroskick, Jon, **Why Do People Vote? A Psychological Analysis of the Causes of Voter Turnout**, Journal of Social Issues, Vol. 64(3), 525-549.

17. Harkins, Stephen and Latane, Bibb, **Population and Political Participation: A Social Impact Analysis of Voter Responsibility**, Group Dynamics: Theory, Research, and Practice, 1998, Vol. 2(3), 192-207.

18. Hertz, Uri, Romand-Monnier, Margaux, Konstantina, Kyriakopoulou & Bhrami, Bahador, **Social Influence Protects Collective Decision Making from Equality Bias**, Journal of Experimental Psychology, American Psychological Association, 2015.

19. Jost, John, Glaser, Jack, Kruglanski, Arie & Sulloway, Frank, **Exceptions that Prove the Rule—Using a Theory of Motivated Social Cognition to Account for ideological Incongruities and Political Anomalies: Reply to Greenberg and Jonas (2003)**, Psychological Bulletin, 2003, Vol. 129(3), 383-393.

20. McCann, Stewart, **Political Conservatism, Authoritarianism, and Societal Threat: Voting for Republican Representatives in U.S. Congressional Elections from 1946-1992**, Journal of Psychology, 2009, Vol. 143(4), 341-358.

21. Milgram, Stanley, **Obedience to Authority: An Experimental Study**, HarperPerennial, N.Y., N.Y., 1974)

22. Obermaier, Magdalena, Koch, Thomas and Baden, Christian, **Everybody Follows the Crowd**, Journal of Media Psychology, Advance online publication, http://d.doi.org/10.1027/1864-1105/a000160, October 28, 2015.

23. Osborne, Danny, Wootton, Liz, & Sibley, Chris, **Are Liberals Agreeable or Not? Politeness and Compassion Differentially Predict Political Conservatism via Distinct Ideologies**, Social Psychology, 2013, Vol. 44(5), pp 353-360.

24. Pacepa, Ion & Rychlak, Ronald, **Disinformation**, WND Books, Washington, D.C., 2013.

25. Rentfrow, Peter, Jokela, Markkus, Gosling, Samuel, Stilwell, David & Kosinski, Michal, **Divided We Stand: Three Psychological Regions of the United States and Their Political, Economic, Social and Health Correlates,** Journal of Personality and Social Psychology, 2013, Vol. 105(6), 996-1012.

26. Rich, Patrick and Zaragoza, Maria, **The Continued Influence of Implied and Explicitly Stated Misinformation in News Reports**, Journal of Experimental Psychology: Learning, Memory & Cognition, 2015, advanced online publication, lhttp://dx.doi.org/10.1037/xlm0000155.

27. Ridout, Tavis & Searles, Kathleen, **It's My Campaign I'll Cry if I Want to: How and When Campaigns Use Emotional Appeals**, Political Psychology, Vol. 32(3), 2011, 439-458.

28. Ringuist, Evan & Dasse, Carl, **Lies, Damned Lies, and Campaign Promises?,** Social Science Quarterly, 2004, Vol. 85(2), 400-419.

29. Schriescheim, Chester, Hinkin, Timothy, Podsakoff, Philip, **Can Ipsative and Single-Item Measures Produce Erroneous Results in Field Studies of French and Raven's (1959) Five Basis of Power?**, Journal of Applied Psychology, 1991, Vol. 76(1), 106-114,

30. Schwartz, Caprara, Gian & Vecchione, Michele, **Basic Personal Values, Core Political Values, and Voting: A Longitudinal Analysis**, Political Psychology, 2010, Vol. 31(3), 1467-2010.

31. Smith, Brandt & Zarate, Michael, **The Effects of Religious Priming and Persuasion Style on Decision-Making in a Resource Allocation Task**, Journal of Peace Psychology, 2015, Advance online publication: http://dx.doi.org/10.1037/pac0000125.

32. Stromwall, Leif & Willen, Rebecca, **Inside Criminal Minds: Offenders Strategies When Lying**, Journal of Investigative Psychology and Offender Profiling, 2011, Vol. 8, 271-181.

33. Tannenbaum, Melanie, Helper, Justin, Zimmerman, Rick, Saul, Lindsey & Jacobs, Samantha, **Appealing to Fear: A Meta-Analysis of Fear Appeal Effectiveness and Theories**, Psychological Bulletin, 2015, Vol. 141(6), 1178-1204.

34. Vecchione, Michele, Caprara, Gianvittorio, Dentale, Francesco & Schwartz, Shalom, **Voting and Values: Reciprocal Effects over Time**, Political Psychology, 2013, Vol. 34(4), 465-485.

35. Winter, David, **Things I've Learned About Personality From Studying Political Leaders at a Distance**, Journal of Personality, 2005, Vol. 73(3), 558-584.

36. Winter, David, **Why Achievement Motivation Predicts Success in Business but Failure in Politics: The Importance of Personal Control**, Journal of Personality, 2010, Vol. 78(6), 1637-1668.

37. Young, Olga, Willer, Robb, & Keltner, Dacher, **"Thou Shalt Not Kill": Religious Fundamentalism, Conservatism, and Rule-Based Moral Processing**, Psychology of Religion and Spirituality, 2013, Vol. 5(2), 110-115.

38. Young, Holly, Rooze, Magda and Holsappel, Jorien, **Translating Conceptualizations Into Practical Suggestions: What the Literature on Radicalization Can Offer to Practitioners**, Peace and Conflict Journal of Peace Psychology, 2015, Vol 21(2), 212-225.

ABOUT THE AUTHOR

Dr. Mel Whitehurst is a psychologist in Plano, Texas. Over the years he worked as a public school counselor, a Director of Counseling and Professor of Human Development at the college level, and for a Fortune 100 company before entering private practice for 27 years. Now "semi-retired", Dr. Whitehurst devotes his time studying how people influence and relate to each other and how the media influences our thinking and behavior. His objective is to develop ideas and provide suggestions that will improve human relationships in the current social media environment.